Acknowledgements

I would like to express a deep gratitude and affection to the people who have had the greatest influence on my personal and spiritual life: my wife Tabot Sandrine Egbe , my dad Tabot Daniel, my mum Oben Mary Tabi, my pastors; Sunday Arokoye and Enow Mbi.

Insight to personal finance has also been deeply influenced by a great and powerful woman Mary Akaya who inspired me to complete this work. Thank you.

A special word of thanks to my wife, Tabot Sandrine Egbe and my think-tank friends; Tankoh Malvin and Achankeng Nico, for editing and reviewing the manuscript.

INTRODUCTION

Finding it difficult to manage your money? Struggling to be an entrepreneur? Why go through hard times when you are able to learn things easier and simpler. Know and understand the money management formulas from the experts.

Financial education is something that everyone needs to know but unfortunately it is not part of our school curriculum. After all, everybody is born to be an entrepreneur, as man is an economic being but the thing is, not everyone knows that. People grow up thinking they are to be somebody's employee someday. We all need to be masters of our personal finance.

It is said that the fundamental law for having financial liberty or freedom is financial education. So we shall be taking a walk in this book to learn about this money management experience.

There are four ways people can earn an income, and these are:

- **Being an employee** – "you have a job". This means you work for somebody else. You were hired by a certain company or business and you work under someone with a position higher than you, or you directly work for the one who owns the company.

    - **Being self-employed** – "you own a job". This means you do not have a boss or a superior;

you do not work in a company. But to earn your salary, you have to offer your services first.

- **Business owner –** "you own a company or system and people work for you". This means you run your own business. You have a company that offers products and services for purchasing.

- **Investor –** "money works for you". You earn by investing your money on to something, like building a restaurant or shopping center.

The first two, being an employee and being self-employed, in order to earn their salary, they need and use time. People who fall under these categories work from time to time to make money.

On the other hand, those people who are business owners or investors use money to make money. Those who have their own businesses use a huge amount of money to build and manage their company. Those who invested on something, also use money to make that investment.

It is essential for every person to be financially literate in order to gain financial liberty. So take time to learn the money management skills.

When you're in your 30s, chances are you're paying your mortgage, getting married, and perhaps even starting a family. Your focus will probably be on ensuring a stable income, getting rid of student loans, and ensuring that you look out for your family's financial future.

Basic Rule: Spend Less Than You Earn!

The fundamental rule of personal finance is **Live within your means**. *If your annual expenditure outweighs your income, you are bound to live a life of misery and unhappiness. At that point you will be living about five years behind time. It is very difficult to find a book or article on personal finance without seeing this fundamental principle pop up. It appears to be a major must in personal financial management.*

Living above your means is like exhaling before you inhale, it can but suffocate you to death. Living and maintaining a life style above your means has a great erosive force on your finance. You will be tied and sunk deep into debts. This has been the major reason for many suicides by flamboyant professionals and business men. The more you struggle to maintain a lifestyle, the deeper into debts you will be as the loan interest forms a part of your monthly expenditure. Your debt will keep compounding and eating up your income until you are completely financially suffocated.

On the other hand if you device ways in which you can save a certain percentage of your income monthly, your savings account will increase and you will be able to earn some interest from the savings. The interest may be too small compared to the enjoyment you should have gotten from consumption but the end result is always amazing. Building wealth is simpler than spending above your income and the advantages are enormous. You will be saved from frequent heart attacks and blood pressures when ever emergency repairs pop up.

The simple strategy for achieving a buoyant financial life is spending less and earning more. In this book, we shall be looking at ways to reduce expenditure and increase earnings and making great savings.

Chapter 1

SAVINGS

The word savings according to the oxford Advanced levels dictionary is defined using three synonyms-Budget, economize, tighten your belt all meaning to spend less money.

To save is to keep money instead of spending it, often in order to buy a particular thing. Here are some saving types, tips and techniques.

CHOOSING A SAVING ACCOUNT- Shocking as it sounds, your savings accounts could actually be losing you money by paying you a rate of interest that's below inflation. For this reason, if you haven't kept an eye on the return you're getting from your saving accounts, it could well be time to move your hard earned cash to a more profitable bank. However, deciding to move is the easy part, choosing a savings account can be trickier. There are such an enormous range of good savings accounts available, for children and adults, that knowing which is right for you isn't always easy. So, to make things a whole lot simpler, I will explain in this book the three fundamental questions that you need to ask when looking for the best savings accounts.

Where can I get the best savings account rates?- This is always the most important question to ask and while it may seem like an obvious one, the answer isn't always as straight forward as it may seem. Getting the best savings account rates isn't always about picking the highest interest savings accounts as, once tax is factored in and bonuses expire, even the best saving account can soon turn into a middling one.

REGULAR SAVINGS ACCOUNTS- In general, regular savings accounts are often the next best place for your money as they often feature headline grabbing savings rates that banks and building societies use to lure in new customers. However, while this type of saving account can give you a really good return they usually come with a whole glut of restrictions that govern how much you can pay in and how you can access your money so it pays to do your research first.

FIXED RATE BONDS- Savings bonds and fixed term accounts usually offer a better return than their instant access counter parts and really attractive rates of interest are available for those who don't mind tying their money up for a while. However, this type of fixed account is only ever worth considering if you are confident that you won't need to access your money as it's likely that interest penalties will be applied if you need to make a withdrawal midterm - this would seriously affect the profitability of even the best savings account.

INSTANT ACCESS SAVINGS ACCOUNTS-
Instant access accounts are next in line and tend to be a much more flexible option as you can get to your money as and when you need it. Compare savings account interest rates and look for the highest return possible but keep an eye out for bonuses that inflate the interest rate for a short while and then drop. If you're happy to move your money regularly then chasing bonus rates can be a very profitable pastime. To do this you'll need to compare savings accounts on a regular basis. If new best buy savings accounts are introduced onto the market and the savings accounts rates and terms and conditions suit, you'll simply need to transfer your money so that you continually profit from the highest interest savings account available.

However, if this sounds like too much effort then a savings account that pays a consistently high rate of interest is likely to be more suitable. Accounts that offer rate guarantees are also a very good bet as they give you the confidence that your money is getting a good return until a certain date in the future.

CHOOSE YOUR ACCESS: While interest rates are an undoubtedly important part of choosing where to domicile your money, it's also important to find a top savings account that's going to let you access your money in a way that suits you. Fixed term options do often offer the best returns (and tend to be available in anything from 6 month to 5 year terms). However, if you are likely to need your money at all during the specified time frame then it's unlikely that this type of account will be worth your while as the interest penalties typically associated with mid-term withdrawal will outweigh any benefit earned from even the best saving accounts.

For this reason, high interest, instant access accounts are usually a good bet if you need to be flexible with your funds. Both taxable and tax-free accounts are available with instant access so you will be spoilt for choice and should base your decision largely on interest rates when comparing them. In addition to this, you'll also need to consider how you want to access your money. If you're affable with your computer then an online savings account is likely to be convenient and providers often offer the best returns over the internet. However, if you value a branch based service then this is something to also look out for, while maximizing your savings is about getting the best return on your money, it's only worth it if you have an account that you feel comfortable operating.

DO I NEED AN INCOME FROM MY SAVINGS?- Many of the top savings accounts only pay interest annually, either on the anniversary of account opening or on some other pre-specified date. However, others allow you to take income from your investment on a monthly basis. Some accounts on the other hand offer both options so that you have the flexibility to choose without compromising on getting the type of account you want. If you're likely to need a monthly income from your saving then this is definitely an important feature to consider when you compare saving accounts.

WHAT NEXT?-Once you've figured out what type of savings account is going to work for you it's simply down to finding an account that matches your criteria, something that using our handy top three savings accounts comparison tables should only take a few minutes at most. However, it is not the final stop point. While it's tempting to sit back and relax once you've made sure that your money is working hard you shouldn't get too comfortable as accounts do change and savings rates do plunge. By keeping an eye on the return your account is providing, taking the time to regularly compare savings accounts interest rates using comparison sites and strategically switching when it stops giving you the best deal, you can make sure that your savings continue to grow as fast as they possibly can indefinitely.

Emergency Fund.

Emergency savings are a lot like medical aid: truly valued when really needed. They are used for precaution and emergency response situations. Alarmingly, when something suddenly happens to you that requires money, you might wish that you had put more money away into an emergency savings account. By then it could be too late.

A recent study reveals that 50 per cent of Americans have a higher amount of money in their emergency savings than the money which was their credit card debt. This is the lowest percentage since the issue was monitored in 2012. Another finding in the report was that 15 per cent of Americans do not have any emergency savings or debt related to credit cards. This shows that the issue is not only that credit card debt is superseding savings, but that even when people do not have credit card debt, many are still not focused on having an emergency hoard of cash should something happen to them.

It's not always easy to think about starting an emergency fund when there are so many other financial obligations to deal with, or maybe you do think about it but you haven't had a chance to start one. Part of the problem is that many people think they need a massive amount of money set aside, but this is not true. By knowing exactly what you should be striving to save, it makes it easier to keep an emergency account versatile for the future.

Here are some tips to help you start saving for emergencies:

You should have between six and eight months of your living expenses saved in this special account. That is the amount to work towards saving. The reason for this amount is that it's not just accidents that can happen but a loss of income, such as if you lose your job or your business crumbles. By knowing how much money you currently use to live comfortably and setting that amount aside, in the event of a sudden halt to your income you would be able to continue your quality of life.

It is advisable to open a separate account for emergencies from your other savings as you don't want the amount to get mixed up in your other savings or used for things that might pop up. Make regular and consistent deposits into this sinking fund account. You are trying to build six to eight months of your expenditure, so with that in your mind, set a plan of how much you will be able to save and stick to it. Make small weekly and monthly amounts that will not immediately have an impact on your lifestyle and watch it grow over time. Once the money has compounded, move it into a higher interest yielding account. You can put it into a convertible investment account.

You will need a great willpower and discipline – have to put aside this sinking fund of cash from your income for other purposes. Thrive to lower your standard of living for the sake of your future. Whenever you receive each paycheck, start off with keeping aside petty amount that is easy to set aside. In less than no time, the sinking fund amount would reach at least 10% of your monthly income. Accumulate this amount to make a "Sinking Fund"

After you fill your Sinking Fund, you don't get any respite continue to save 15% of your income with a goal that the accumulated excess cash will be invested. The goal is to invest in something that benefits you during difficult times or when an important need arises.

We're always being encouraged to save money, whether that is by creating a savings account or keeping tabs on our spending habits. However, there are some savings myths that could be doing your money more harm than good. Here are some to check out and lose:

Avoid Impulse Buying-Impulse spending can make it almost impossible for someone to manage their finances effectively. It creates a habitual need to spend and a knee-jerk reaction to sales, products, and advertising. And the result is usually the same: a lack of cash flow, problems saving, and almost always an inability to maintain a budget.

First, impulse spending is almost always chronic and recurring. To see something every once in a while and "splurge" is normal. Impulse spending is something that happens regularly and develops into a bad habit.

Second, buying on an impulse means that you're making an unplanned purchase that you hadn't already recognized a need for. These purchases might be useful and might even seem wise on the surface, but had you not made visual contact with the item, you probably wouldn't have wanted to spend money on it. In other words, an impulse purchase is made when a product or ad instigates the transaction. Instead of you deciding that you need something and then going to find it, you see a product or service and decide immediately that it warrants your money. Those who struggle with this end up spending a lot of money that they didn't need to spend or that wouldn't have been spent, had they been in control of their purchases. In fact, that's the real goal here — to be in control of how you make purchases.

    Impulse spending is a habit, so try breaking it by avoiding all discretionary spending. That's not to say that you can't pick back up after a few weeks, but stick to essentials until you've given yourself enough time to get comfortable spending money on just those things.

    The goal is to take away your tendency to be a reactive purchaser, before you take the steps necessary to build yourself back into a proactive budgeter. Once you can go into stores and see ads without feeling that tremble making you want to spend money, you're ready to move on. It'll happen quicker than you think.

The underlying problem with impulse spending is that you end up losing control of your money. If products, services or advertisements are completely driving you to spend, then you'll never be able to stop, because those things will always be there. While it's true that those things have an informative impact (i.e. you see a product and can tell it's useful), the bulk of the decision should stem from your own needs and decisions. Thus, learning how to avoid impulse buys will go a long way to protect your finances.

Pay your debts and save simultaneously- Some people suggest that paying off your debts is the most important thing, while others insist that you should be saving. The truth is that both of these should be done simultaneously. Have money deposited from your income into an investment account the minute it comes into your savings. In this way, you don't put all your eggs in one basket and you can tie up some funds into an investment before spending opportunities come knocking. This gives you a better shot at saving because if all you are doing is trying to pay off your debts, you won't have emergency savings at your disposal should something come up.

Learn to save more with the smallest Income-Although it might feel that you don't have much money to save with your current earnings, chances are that if you earned more money it would be allocated to things other than saving. The truth is that you can try to save with whatever you have, even if that means only a tiny portion of your monthly income goes to your savings. Although everyone wishes to save a large amount of money every month, this is not really possible - irrespective of how much income is coming in. Try to save on one thing - that could be cancelling a club membership that you don't even use or not giving into impulse buying - and you will see that you can achieve quite a bit with what you have. If you waste time waiting to earn more money to save, and then you won't be saving at all which is much worse than saving small amounts at a time.

Get all members of your household to start the saving culture-This can be done by creating a decorative change jar to keep in your home, allowing everyone in the household the opportunity to deposit their change to save for a rainy day. Another option is to save all of your $5-$10 bills whenever you come into possession of one. If every time you break a bill and get a $5-$10to put away you will see that in no time you have a substantial savings right there in your home.

If it feels that you hardly see your money before it gets allotted to a bill or service, then it's a good idea to open a savings account into which you can save whatever bit you can when you get paid every month. This prevents you from needing this money for something else because it is immediately out of sight. Even if the money you're saving is not a lot, you are still young enough to start accumulating a nice bundle of cash that could come in handy on a rainy day.

Sell Things You Don't Need-You probably have accumulated some things that you don't even use anymore, such as evocative items from your younger days. When combining your life with that of a partner, really think hard about what you both want for this new phase of your life. It's probably much less than you think. Hold a garage sale or go online to sites like eBay where you can get rid of items and make some extra money from selling them that you can later save.

Save Your Salary Increases-It's a great feeling to earn more money in your career, but avoid the temptation of letting this money go to your lifestyle, such as in the form of a new car, entertainment, holidays and so on. Of course you want to enjoy life, but that doesn't mean the entire amount has to disappear. Save as much of your increase as you can. Pretend you don't have it since you were managing before it just fine, after all. After a few months of saving your increase, it will feel so good that you'll definitely want to continue saving more.

Buy, Don't Rent-Although renting might seem to be more practical, it can waste money in the long-term. Owning your own home helps you save money because a fixed-rate mortgage won't mean that you have to worry about things such as increases as you would if you're renting a place. Added to this, you will eventually pay your mortgage and this will allow you to have more money at your disposal when you retire.

Save money when Buying Investment Property- When most people think of money-saving tips, they think of how to save on food, utilities, and discretionary purchases. But there are also ways to save money when buying investment property.

The most important task is to do your research first and make sure that you're financially ready for the risk that investment properties bring. You also need to consider all expenses involved, including purchase cost and loan amount, and costs of carrying the property, such as taxes and insurance. Before you start looking, define why you want to buy investment property. Is it for an extra income stream? To eventually quit your job and make your living from investment property? To have a more comfortable retirement?

Your reason for buying an investment property will influence your choices along the way. Knowing your reasons helps you stay focused. Then, when it's time to start scoping out properties, consider these money saving ideas that can help.

Start as Owner-Occupant-With this strategy; you buy a property to live in that you will later rent out. If you occupy a house for at least a year or until you repay the loan on which you used to pay for the house, you can make a smaller down payment, particularly with VA -approved properties. After you have lived in the house for at least two years, you find another house to purchase and move into, and rent out the original house. Douse and replicate as desired. The obvious drawback to this approach is the hassle of frequent moves, particularly if you have young children. Make sure you and your partner are fully on board with owner-occupancy before trying it.

Ask the Seller to Pay Closing Costs-One of the more common money saving tips when buying real estate is asking the seller to help with closing costs. Seller financing may be rare, but you may be able to get the seller to pay for part of the closing costs as a condition of your offer.

Buyers often ask for a percentage of the closing costs to be paid by sellers. Sometimes sellers who won't come down on the price will agree to cover some of the closing costs in order to get their asking price. Don't be afraid to ask. Worst case is they'll say no and you start negotiations over.

If you're considering buying investment property, it is critical to think of it as a long-term investment. Even in the prime of property flipping before the real estate meltdown, flipping a property required a lot of hard work, more work than most people realized.

If you can follow some of these money-saving tips, break even on the expenses and keep the property in repair, it should gain value over time. You should be prepared for the responsibilities of a landlord (or hire a top property manager to do it for you), and you need to be able to financially withstand a one or two month vacancy if the rental market is slow in your area.

Investment properties can be a terrific investment, or they can be disastrous. Knowing the market, your own risk level, and the level of work required is essential to succeeding as a real estate investor.

*Chapter **Two***

Expense Management

How often do you hear people talk about how they would live their dreams if they only had a bit more money? People always dream about moving to a remote area or about staying home with the kids or about relocating to the bug out location, but often feel that these things are financially unreachable. Do you do this yourself?

If so, then maybe it's time to take a good hard look at your personal finances and enact a personal austerity plan. Most people would be surprised at the changes that can be made when they rethink the definition of the word "necessities". It is time for us to take some moments out and redefine necessities.

If your finances are out of control, the best possible reality check is a bleak look at what necessities really are. It is not necessary in life to have an iPAD, a vehicle in both car parks of your car garage, or for your children to all have separate bedrooms. With many people all over the world scrambling for food, basic medications like aspirin, and shelter, these necessities are those things essential to life:

- Water
- Food (and the ability to cook it)
- Medicine and medical supplies
- Basic hygiene supplies
- Shelter (including sanitation, lights, heat)
- Simple tools
- Seeds
- Defense Items

Utterly everything above those basic necessities is a luxury. It all depends on your immediate need. So, by this definition, what luxuries do you have?

Some are more important than others, based on your lifestyle and might be considered secondary necessities. You might require transportation, work clothing, a computer and an internet connection, electrical appliances, a cell phone – you are the only person who can define which are these are luxuries and which are secondary necessities. It's essential to be truly honest with yourself and separate "wants" and "I really enjoy having this" and "the kids will complain without it" from "needs"

For example, if you are a Banker or an Accountant or you a customer service job, you need to get a perfect wardrobe and great perfumes as opposed to a freelance writer who needs an internet connection and a laptop for his job. For a freelance writer to make a living, therefore, his computer and monthly internet bill are a necessity. However, because he works from home, a fashionable work wardrobe may not important to him.

One of the biggest challenges in personal finance is figuring out ways to reduce the regular bills that eat up your monthly budget. These continuous regular expenses simply fill up our budget, leaving us less money to invest for the future – and also less money to spend on things that we enjoy.

With the gloomy economic forecast, it's not reasonable or rational to expect things to improve in the near future. If you want to be somewhat immune to the financial difficulties coming down the pipe, you need to perform a financial makeover to pare down the monthly output to the bare minimum.

Does this sound kind of grim? It's not – decreasing your monthly output provides a different kind of safety net. You can end (or at least reduce) your slavery to the system, where the government helps itself to at least 30% of your paycheck through payroll deductions. With your newfound freedom, you may discover that you have the money to start a business, relocate, or cut back your work hours to spend more time doing the important things in life.

Devastating financial changes are coming to a location near you. Wouldn't you prefer to make the cuts now and adjust accordingly, instead of having them forced upon you through evictions, foreclosures, repossessions, and other painful methods?

Design Your Own Personal Austerity Plan

It is so important to make changes in your personal finance because your life style is based on either the economic climate of your employer, your business or the economy in which you reside in. So if you don't change your way of life, the government or your company will. A salary cut will. A job loss will. Inflation will.

When cuts are made, the "Powers That Be" make sure to devise it so that those cuts affect the average person – the voters. They can make it hurt, then swoop in and "rescue" us, by further enslaving us.

These upcoming cuts won't hurt the ones who are making the cuts. Parliamentarians and company directors will still get large salaries and raises. The wives of executives will still spend millions of taxpayer monies on vacations that would make the common man redden. The presidential villa will still serve epicurean meals while average citizens are digging through the garbage to stave off hunger.

Pragmatically speaking, the way things are going, none of us is likely to get a robust raise. We'll be lucky to keep the incomes we have if not experience a decrease. But expenses are only going to increase exponentially. To keep the true necessities within reach, we need to reduce our expenditures and put away emergency funds.

Personal bank accounts are being plundered across the globe. People are not just living paycheck to paycheck – The take home pay can no longer take them home. Most people are living hand to mouth, scavenging what they can in order to stay out of hunger.

Making some difficult changes now can provide a stable standard of living in a world that is going downhill at swift speed. By decreasing your monthly output, you can hang on to necessities. I'd rather choose my own austerity plan than to have it forced upon me.

This is where the brutal cuts come in. What can you change about your life? Where can you reduce expenditures by several thousand dollars monthly? This is the point at which most people say, "I can't." Most people don't want to move to a smaller house, get an old car, or go without premium cable. But this is where you can truly dig in and change your life.

As I mentioned before, everyone's situation is different. You may be locked into a mortgage on a huge house in a market that won't even cover the balance of what you owe. It could be the same with your vehicle. Explore all of your options, though, because paying a few thousand dollars to get out from under it could be worthwhile. Some people could have reached the point where they must begin to default on payments. That too, is a personal choice. I'm not recommending that you change your obligations. (However, do consider the fact that large banks get bailed out by the government, and the citizens do not.) Before making decisions like that, be sure to discover all of the potential ramifications, such as repossessions, trimming of bank accounts, and busted credit.

Here are a few Austerity measures you may apply, divided up into several sensible categories.

The best approach for cutting required spending is to simply walk through all of the required expenses and look for ways to lower each.

Vehicle Expenses

Automobiles are sinking holes for money – they create leakages for money to be evaporated at very fast rates. They are constantly devalued, gulp down fuel by each turning of wheel, and constantly require repairs and maintenance work. How can we reduce the cost of automobiles in our monthly budget?

Share a Ride - If you have an opportunity to carpool with a colleague or friend to and from work, that will not only significantly reduce the depreciation of your car and gas expenses, it will also reduce your car maintenance cost. You and your colleague can choose a day in the week to use each other's car so that no one should feel cheated.

Use public transportation-If you have an option that enables you to ride to regular destinations (such as work, the store, or a shopping center) instead of using your automobile, you can save quite a bit of money on gas and maintenance by just dropping a few coins on the bus or the rail system and leaving the car at home (or parking it at a station). You may as well take a walk to nearby destinations, this will also help save some fitness club bills and get you healthy.

Sell/tradeoff an automobile-*If an automobile is sitting in your car park and isn't used, consider selling it. If nothing else, the insurance expense will go away, and if you can use the money from the sale to pay it off or, better yet, pocket some of the money, even better. You can as well sell or trade off your large luxurious car for a small low cost efficient one.*

Keep the tires on your automobiles properly inflated-*Once a week, stop by a local gas station that offers free air and check the air pressure in your car tires, and then fill each one to the maximum recommended amount as stated in your manual. This improves gas mileage by one percent for every two PSI of air you are able to add to your tires.*

DEBT REDUCTION

The higher your debt, the bigger the cost of refinancing the debt and its corresponding interest. Interest payments constitute a major part of our monthly expense. Any opportunity you have to reduce your debt will obviously help in your monthly payments, but many people don't have the cash available to eliminate debt. There are other options for reducing your monthly debt load

Refinance your home and/or automobile-Contact some lending institutions and inquire about rates. You might be able to get into a situation that reduces your monthly debt payments without significantly increasing your overall cost in the long term.

Consolidate your loans-Don't hold out for a hope of better rates to consolidate your loans, especially if your current rates are quite high. Spend the time to find a good loan consolidation option and it will pay off every single month. Pool all your loans into a single debt basket with the best conditions. More so you may get a small personal loan through your local credit union. This is a great option if you've borrowed money to make a smaller purchase, such as furniture or a small home improvement project, and you're finding the interest rates uncomfortable. The perfect place to look for a helping hand here is your local credit union, which will often offer small personal loans at a nice rate if your credit is solid.

Request a credit card rate reduction- *If you've got a decent amount on your credit card, call up your credit card company and request a rate reduction. If they won't go for it, get a 0% balance transfer onto another card. The input here, though, is to* STOP BUYING ON CREDIT UNTIL YOUR FINANCIAL SITUATION IS HEALTHY.

Sign up for automatic debt repayment plans- *Many installment plans, particularly those with student loans, offer an interest rate reduction if you sign up for an automatic plan. You should never pass these up – not only do they save money automatically each month, they're also incredibly convenient. If you have any installment payments (particularly student loan debt), see if such an offer is available to you*

Energy Bills

We all face a continual onslaught of energy costs, especially as we use more and more electronic devices. Luckily, technology has brought us a few effective ways to reduce costs as well. Compact fluorescent light bulbs are receiving a big push right now and their advantages are great: a longer lifespan and significantly less electrical usage. Stick with the name brands for now, even at a premium: when comparing bulbs, use the *LUMENS* number to compare bulbs, not the equivalent wattages – the *LUMENS* indicate the actual amount of light emitted by the bulb. Remember also that under normal usage (4 hours a day) and normal electrical rates ($0.10 per kilowatt hour), replacing a 75 watt bulb with a 20 watt CFL saves $0.66 per month. Multiply that by all the bulbs in your house to see how much you'll save every month.

Install a *programmable thermostat*- *A programmable thermostat allows you to automatically alter the heating and cooling of your home when you're not at home, when you're asleep, and so on, saving significantly on your heating and cooling bills.*

Unplug all unused electrical devices- *Are there any electrical devices around the house that stay plugged in, but that you rarely use? Most electric devices use a small amount of electricity constantly, a* PHANTOM *charge. To eliminate that usage, unplug the items.*

Along those lines, consider utilizing power strips and power timers to turn electrical devices on and off. A power strip with a switch on it, when turned off, blocks the phantom charge on those devices; a timer can automatically turn off the charge going to a power strip (or anything plugged into it) at a certain time each night. This is a great way to eliminate phantom charge on your home electronic equipment at night.

Install a blanket for your hot water heater and reduce the temperature-*In many homes, the hot water heater is a major energy drain; the water is kept hotter than most people ever use, plus the heat is constantly lost to the environment, meaning you have to burn more energy than ever to keep the water so hot. Solve both problems by dropping the temperature down to 125-130 degrees Fahrenheit (around 60 degrees Celsius) and also installing a blanket on your water heater to keep in the heat – a blanket can pay for itself in about a year.*

Entertainment Expenses

Many people look at entertainment as the first thing to cut when trying to trim costs, but they often forget to look at the regular expenditures that slowly eat away at your finances month in and month out. Here are some things to consider that you may have overlooked before.

Cancel club memberships- Look at things like a health club, a country club, golf club, tennis club and so on. How often do you really use these services? If you're using a gym membership less than once a week or a country club membership less than once a month, you're likely throwing away money.

Reduce or eliminate your cable bill- For many people, this advice is beyond the pale, but it's worth looking at. Perhaps you could trim back on your premium channel selection and just go with basic cable, or perhaps you could even eliminate your cable bill entirely – it will also help with electricity costs because you won't be watching television as much and you'll suddenly find you have much more free time. You may get a cable dish that offers mostly free channels.

Look for inexpensive entertainment options- Do you utilize the community library? Do you attend local community events like municipal band concerts and so on? Are you aware of local volunteer groups and organizations? Your community often offers many options for inexpensive or free entertainment of all kinds – you don't have to have a big entertainment budget each month.

Strongly reduce or eliminate travel- *If you live very far from your extended families, you will be aware of the costs of travel. Being selective about where you travel to – and also open to inviting people to visiting you – you will significantly cut down on travel expenses.*

Cancel newspaper and magazine subscriptions- *If you get a magazine or newspaper in the mail but simply don't read it, cancel that subscription when it comes up for renewal no matter how much you "like" the magazine. An unread subscription is nothing more than expensive litter.*

Food Bills

Make the kitchen your favorite room in the house, though it may seem more convenient to eat out to many people, it's incredibly expensive and not as much of a time saver as you might think. Consider these options;

Cook (and pack) your own meals at home- *When you cook at home, make plenty so that you can freeze some of it for future meals and, even better, take some of it as leftovers to work, drastically reducing the cost of the typical workplace lunch.*

Reduce or eliminate eating out or getting take-out-
Take-out and dining out can be a huge timesaver for a busy family, but the expense can be tremendous and it often doesn't save much time, either. Instead, look at other options for dining at home: prepare lots of meals at once and freeze them for easy cooking later, focus on simple recipes, and choose recipes that utilize the fresh produce in season in your area.

Consider before you order- You could avoid eating out altogether, but that provides an opportunity for you to socialize with friends and family. So, what do you do? You certainly don't need to go hungry. Portion sizes are increasing at restaurants. Often, you'll get more food than you could ever eat. Consider ordering as small as possible. Stick to the main course as appetizers, desserts and alcoholic drinks are the big profit categories for most restaurants. Drinks of any kind will add a couple of dollars to your bill. By some estimates, a $2 glass of iced tea actually costs the business two cents. That's an enormous profit margin that will cost you. A glass of water is not only better for you, but it could easily save you $25 a month, too.

Buy nonperishable items in bulk- Many people never even bother to look at some of the larger packages of nonperishable items – they think it's just too much. Try looking at the cost per unit of all of the sizes and choose the one that's the best deal; often, it is the big bulky package, but that just means you won't be buying it again for a long time. Spread out over months and over a lot of items (think of all of the nonperishable's in your home – food is just the beginning), this can add up to a lot of trimmed plump.

Start a garden- Vegetable gardening is a splendid hobby that can often turn a profit if done well. Focus on vegetables that are easy to grow and produce abundant fruit, like tomatoes, and learn how to store the excess through such processes as canning. Opening up a jar of tomatoes in the winter that were grown by you in the summer and canned in the fall is a wonderful experience and it can really help with trimming the food bill.

Avoid Buying Branded Products- Many products (not just food) are available in a store-brand or generic form for significantly less money – quite often with the name brand, you're paying for their advertising budget with the higher cost. Look carefully at the ingredients in generic and name-brand products and if they're the same, go with the generic one on a regular basis, which will consistently trim money from your shopping bill.

Insurance Bills

We all have insurance to protect against the unexpected, but when we overpay for insurance, we leave ourselves vulnerable in a different way by stretching our budget too thin. Look into these options for ways to reduce your insurance premiums.

Downgrade your health insurance- *Ask at work about the various options available to you that might reduce your insurance costs, and don't neglect to look into family options if you have children – if you do, all working members of the household should look at family coverage.*

Go With Cash

It's kind of an old-school approach to cutting expenses, so old that some people have forgotten about it. Maybe it's time to bring back the envelope system. Once you're organized, you can divide your paycheck by category: entertainment, gasoline and food, for example. Decide how much money you're willing and able to spend for each category. Put that amount of cash in the correspondingly addressed envelope. When your entertainment cash is gone you can't swipe a debit or credit card. If you've nearly spent the cash in your gasoline folder, you avoid taking that last-minute excursion out of town.

How does the envelope system cut your monthly expenses? By erasing the illusion created by that plastic in your wallet that there's always a little extra that can be spent. An envelope doesn't have an expanding and tempting credit limit. When it's empty, it's empty.

People who pay with cash say there's a psychological incentive to spend less. Handing over the actual money you earned is tougher than swiping a debit or credit card. In fact, some say it hurts to take that money out of a purse or wallet and say goodbye to it. Paying with cash, you're more likely to make a smaller purchase or skip it altogether.

Organize

Imagine you're in a yacht that's quickly taking on water. You're sinking. Yes, you have to bail out the water but unless you want to keep bailing indefinitely, you're going to need to find the source of the leak. The same is true with your monthly budget. If you want to eliminate overdraft charges from your bank, late fees on bills and snowballing interest on debt, you have to get organized.

Take the time to write out all your monthly expenditures and all your sources of income. If you have a clear picture of what you're dealing with, your boat will take on less water. Then you can begin the bailing process, having confidence and peace of mind about the stability of your vessel.

You've undoubtedly heard it said that necessity is the mother of invention. This maxim certainly applies to finances. When times are tough, people invent all kinds of ways to save a buck. They may have already considered themselves to be quite thrifty but suddenly, in the face of absolute necessity, they discover that they didn't truly know what thriftiness was. You invent some cost cutting approaches, your neighbor invents others and when everyone shares their insights, there are a multitude of opportunities to consider.

But just as there are many ways to save money, there are as many (or more) opportunities to waste it. A bounced check, an impulse buy or a holiday shopping spree can erase all of your hard-earned gains. That's why it's important to look, not just at the little things that can be tweaked in your budget, but at your overall approaches to personal finance

Chapter three

Making Budgets

Budgeting lies at the foundation of every financial plan. It doesn't matter if you're living paycheck to paycheck or earning six-figures a year, you need to know where your money is going if you want to have a knob on your finances. Unlike what you might believe, budgeting isn't all about restricting what you spend money on and cutting out all the fun in your life. It's really about understanding how much money you have, where it goes, and then planning how to best allocate those funds. Here's everything you need to help you create and maintain a budget.

Do you know why a budget is so important? On the surface it seems like creating a budget is just a tedious financial exercise, especially if you feel your finances are already in good order. But you might be surprised at just how valuable a budget can be. A good budget can help keep your spending on track and even uncover some hidden cash flow problems that might free up even more money to put toward your other financial goals

Making - and sticking to - a budget is the essential tool for ensuring that our money gets used the way we need it to. Even if you're in the happy situation of having plenty of income, the homework involved in drawing up a budget can be instructive, since you may find that you are spending more than you wish on items that are petty and luxurious like DVDs, electronic gadgetry or restaurant meals.

Drawing up a budget is usually pure hard work enlivened only by the reality of staring your foolish spending habits in the face. Why do you have a luxury sound system if neither you nor your spouse listens to it? In fact, one of the chief impediments to budgeting is that most people would rather not know how they really use their money.

It's bad enough to learn this kind of information on your own. It's even worse when a spouse or significant other finds out, since it usually confirms his or her worst fears - and provides new bullets for future discussions.

Don't worry. Any spending mistakes you're making are probably common and not impossible to lash out. Moreover, the bulk of budgeting's pains are at the beginning.

After you have a budget in place - and you've fine-tuned it with a couple of months of actual spending - tracking your expenditures becomes almost automatic.

The simplest way to track your spending, especially your cash, is the low-tech way, with a notebook and a pen. By carrying around the notebook with you, you can track exactly where every dollar is going–from a small coffee on your way to work to a spending splurge at the mall. If you'd prefer, on a daily or weekly basis, you can transfer your handwritten notes to a computer spreadsheet.

Once you have collected information for about a month, you'll have a good baseline of information to use to create your personal budget. Some major categories that you'll want to include are housing, utilities, insurance, food (groceries and dining out), gasoline, clothing, entertainment, and "other". Using a spreadsheet program (such as Excel), online service, or other personal finance program, add up the expenses that you've been tracking, and then calculate what you'd like to budget for each category. Keep in mind that you'll need to budget for some items, like gifts and automobile repairs, which will be necessary but won't occur every month. You can either create a budget for each individual month, with variances for irregular expenses (e.g., heating expenses which will be higher in winter months, or car repairs and gifts), or a standard monthly budget where you include an average amount for expenses such as car repairs, heating, and gifts.

May be you are a financial planner or a practicing Accountant, if your boss at work were to ask you for an analysis of the department's spending, you'd figure it out quickly enough. It is of absolute importance to have a business mentality when approaching budgeting for your household. A variety of electronic tools can also make the process easier. Below is a rule of the thump on how to create a master budget for your family.

Spend no more than 50% of your after-tax income on fixed expenses, which are anything you *have to* pay for each month, and cannot cut back in the short run. This includes your rent or mortgage, any car payments, basic food, basic utilities, insurance, etc. These are called "Must-Haves". Start by saving at least 20% of your after-tax income every month.

And the rest of the money can be spent on anything you'd like. This is your discretionary spending, for example eating out, a new dress, a big screen TV, anything you'd like-"Wants".

If saving 20% *every* month seems very hard, or impossible, to you, this is probably because you are spending much too much on Must-Haves. The most important single piece of advice in personal finance is to cut your Must-Haves to under 50% of your after-tax income. If this means selling your new SUV and Honda Accord, and buying two 10 year Toyota corolla, then that's what you must do. It will be well worth it to stop constant financial stress (and possibly ruin), and constantly denying yourself the little day-to-day pleasures, to pay hundreds of extra dollars each month to your cars.

If it means selling a home you can't truly afford, then you just have to do it, and move to a smaller one, or a less fancy neighborhood, until you save enough that you can really afford it without constant financial stress, deprivation, and danger of ruin. Your Must-Haves must be brought under 50% of your after-tax pay. The little things like clipping coupons, bringing a bag lunch, etc. are good, but they are just dwarfed by the big fixed expenses – These have got to be dealt with, and eventually cut to less than 50% of your after-tax pay.

With Must-Haves under 50%, if a crisis hits, like losing your job, you have over 50% of your spending (and saving) that can still be cut back immediately, as only Must-Haves are not immediately cut-able. This means that you may be able to weather the storm just on the income of a spouse, or unemployment compensation, without destroying your savings, and after that falling into a ruinous debt spiral.

An important note on Must-Haves is that although they should essentially never exceed 50% of your after tax income, the riskier your income, and life in general, the lower they should be. For example, if you are self employed, and there is a substantial risk of business going bad and your income dropping in half, your Must-Haves should be much lower than 50% so that if this does happen you can weather it without destroying your savings, and then descending into a spiral of debt leading to ruin.

If you have children and a mortgage, you are unfortunately usually more at risk financially; if things go wrong, you are not some 25 year old who can easily ask his landlord to find a new tenant, and then bunk with a friend, or move back in with parents.

And the older you get, typically, the more specialized and high income your job gets. Unfortunately, this usually makes it much more likely that if you lose your job, you won't be able to find another one paying nearly as much. As a result, for most people it makes sense to lower your Must-Haves by about 5% relative to your income every 10 years, at least until your Must-Have percentage is in the 30's.

A great way to do this is, when it does make sense to buy a home, you obtain a fixed payment mortgage. That way, as your income goes up, your mortgage stays the same, lowering your Must-Have percentage. It is also always a great idea for financial security to pay off your mortgage as quickly as possible.

Everyone hates budgeting, but it's a necessary evil. I've tried many strategies for simplifying the process and putting together spending plans I can actually stick to. Here's something I've learned: When building any sort of budget, remember these rules.

Identify your goals- I call this the budget objectives, setting these objectives will enable you have a perfect budget strategy. Think of the following goals; what are your financial goals? Do you have debts you need to pay off? Do you want to minimize the debt you graduate with? Are you trying to save for a car, a vacation, or your future? Budgeting involves tough choices, but having a goal will make budgeting a little less agonizing.

Get Tracking. Do you check your bank account at the end of the month or semester and wonder where all the money went? Before you can manage your money, you have to know how you're spending it. Use a simple tailored spreadsheet to track and categorize your expenses for one month. Get in the habit of recording your expenditures once a day.

It's useful to separate your expenses into three categories:

1. Fixed Needs – Necessary expenses that stay the same from month to month, e.g., rent, phone bill

2. Variable Needs – Necessary expenses that may vary from month to month, e.g., gas, food

3. Wants – Nonessential expenses, e.g., lattes, movies, eating out, electronics

Is this just another rote exercise in organization and formatting? No! Categorizing your expenses will help you balance your budget by identifying which expenditures should be cut back on first.

If you have a monthly savings goal (and you should!), include it as an expense. It is much easier to save money if you've planned for it in your budget. And it's important, too: if you run into unforeseen expenses, you'll want to be able to pay them without going into debt. And even if nothing goes wrong, having some savings will help you follow your dreams in the future.

Focus on Savings- **By now, you've set up your budget. You know how much money you have. But you could still use some help staying on budget. Determine the amount of your budget that you can afford to save each month. Have it direct-deposited to your savings accounts, or to your mutual fund. Wherever you decide to keep your savings, make sure you put money into it every month. That savings will make a big difference for you later.**

Use Cash-Take out enough cash to last one week at a time. Make up your mind that the cash you have is all you get for discretionary expenses or things that you could live without, each week. It's much easier to turn down a $50 pair of shoes when it will take the last of your week's cash than it is when you just have to swipe a credit card.

Cut Bad Habits- Whether it's alcohol or tobacco, if you use much of either, you know how expensive bad habits can be. Stop smoking and drinking, and put the beer/cigarette money toward your other expenses. You'll see your expenses come down -- and feel your health improve -- in no time. You'll also save on medical expenses down the road, and you may become eligible for lower insurance premiums.

Share the Responsibility- Make sure you're not the only member of your household concerned about your budget. If you're working hard to save money, but your spouse and kids are out spending you into debt, you're fighting a losing battle. Sit down together and make a plan to determine how much - spending money you should each have. Then, check in every week to see how well you're doing. If the entire family shares the responsibility for the budget, everyone can cut back just a little and make a big difference. One person shouldn't have to shoulder the entire burden alone.

Keep Your Receipts- You probably monitored your expenses for several weeks to make a budget. Once the budget is made, though, it can be tempting to stop keeping up with every little expense. But keeping track really can help you stick to your budget. Save your receipts, and write down the places you spend money. You'll be less likely to overspend if you realize how much money has actually gone through your hands.

Balance Your Checkbook- Do you balance your checkbook regularly? If not, it's a good habit to start. If you're on a tight budget, a couple of small mistakes can lead to overdraft charges and insufficient funds in your account. If you balance up every time you get a bank statement, you can make sure your ledger never moves to red.

Be Flexible- Remember that life is unpredictable, and things happen that are out of our control. When you make a budget, try to allow some extra money for discretionary expenses and, be gentle with yourself if you go over your budget sometimes. It can be hard to get back on track if you let yourself get too frustrated over a mistake or two.

Forget perfection. A budget is simply a target. Your spending likely won't be perfect the first month (or the second, or the third). If you can't get your money into perfect balance, get it as close as you can. Make adjustments as needed.

Make plans based on reality, not on your idealized life. Don't base your budget on wishful thinking. Sure, you still may get that pay raise or bonus, but wait until it's actually in hand before accounting for it.

Keep it simple. If your system of budgeting is a chore, you'll never follow through. Track by only as much detail as you need. Even if you are able to keep your spending in check, overly complex budgets will fail, because they require too much effort to maintain.

Following these tips can help you stick to your budget. You can prepare for a major purchase without having to borrow more than is absolutely necessary, and you can feel good about keeping your finances under control. Make sure you update your budget regularly, and prioritize your spending -- know what is important enough to be worth your hard-earned money. Budgeting will come more easily the longer you stay with it, and you will reap the rewards in years to come. Above all, remember that budgeting is worth the effort. Keeping on budget can make your entire life run more smoothly, since so many things are affected by your financial status.

Chapter four
Debt Management

The big lesson of many lives has been this: Regardless of how upper-middle class we appear, as long as we have debt we are actually poor. That's kind of the definition of poverty right? Not having money. So, as long as we have debt, we not only have any money, we've got less than no money. I don't see the point in extending our poverty for one day longer than we need to. You may have got five years to pay off your Home Equity Line of Credit. But why extend your poverty for half a decade when you could save three years of financial stress and pay off the debt in one or two years.

The latest Federal Reserve statistics and other governmental institutions data have shown that the average household credit card debt for over 50% of U.S. citizens has reached an outstanding number of $15,252, with an increase of 1.8% from 2014. This being said, more than half of the American population is struggling with paying of credit cards, mortgages and student loans. This statement is true for all nations.

Even if there are those who prefer to live in debt denial and consider having debt a natural part of their lives, the truth is completely different. Some believe they will never be able to repay all their loans, but maintain their living standards, while others are selling their assets to get out of this straining financial situation.

For those who are trying to regain their financial stability and freedom, good news comes their way. There are several steps to becoming debt free, just try and see the results for yourself. Yes, the time in which every dollar will be completely paid off may differ from person to person, but this is strictly dependent on the amount of money they owe and their dedication to this mission.

Analyze Your Monthly Income and Expenses -In all my steps to becoming debt free, this may be the hardest step to take. It requires complete sincerity and a proper evaluation of one's needs and wants. Most indebted citizens take part in the consumerism trend that has been growing exponentially over the last 2 decades, all around the world. In the first instance, if you have a family, involve every member in your quest to escape from debt. Often, parents find it challenging to say "NO" to their children when they make outrageous and impulse demands, but they will be surprised to see the ability of kids to understand and accept changes in their lifestyle, as long as solid arguments are being offered and the situation is explained properly.

Sitting down and analyzing the monthly income and expenses is essential, if you want to be successful in getting rid of loans. It is mandatory to make the difference between "I need" and "I want". Take the time to look around your home and see how many of the last month's purchases are being used on a daily, or even weekly basis. The rest is all money thrown away. You need to sit and make an austerity plan for all members of the family considering their participation- this I call activity based planning. Even if it sometimes seems hard to prepare a meal from scratch, it is usually 50% cheaper than take-out. So the time invested in this type of activities could help you NOT to take a second job or work over time. Saving up is usually the best way to get rid of debt. See chapter two on how to make savings.

Understand Your Loans, Debts Balances and Interest Rates- Take the time to sit down and list all your debts, whether they are credit cards, student loans, mortgages, medical expenses and loans from friends or family members. After you make sure you have not forgotten everything, take out your loan contracts or visit the bank or loaner's website to write down their interest rates (APR) and the balances to which they are addressed. Also, it is important to know the minimum monthly payments required on each credit card or loan. Also, now is the time to combine above points and see how much money you can afford to redirect, on a monthly basis, from your "needs and wants" category to your repayment category. It is advisable to save a small amount of money, each month, for unexpected situations; still, the remaining amount should all be paid back to your creditors.

Choose the Repayment Strategy and Stick with It- After a proper analysis of the debt balance and interest rates to each of them, a choice appears. One is to apply for a consolidation loan. Most financial advisors recommend this method, because it makes it easier for the person with debt to track their payments and to commit to them. Consolidation loans are simply a way of refinancing all your debts into a single one. For those who are granted (a few, though), this method works because it lowers interest rates.

For example: the average interest rate for a credit card can reach 25% annually, while some consolidation loans offer interest rates as low as 15%. This means that if you have 3 maxed out credit cards with a limit of $10,000 each; your total debt reaches $30,000. If each of them has an APR of 25%, the total interest paid during an entire year is $7,500. A consolidation loan of $30,000, with an APR of 15% creates a total amount of interest paid in one year of only $4,500. The remaining $3,000 is what you save.

Still, there is a downside to consolidation loans. As credit scores for people with loans reach alarming low levels, the financial institutions often deny applications. It is a matter of trust and if you consider this as a way to repay your loans, boosting your credit score is necessary before applying for a consolidation loan.

The second method used successfully by many is to pay off balances from highest to lowest interest rates. You can be tempted to first pay off the bigger loan to quick run away from debt but usually, bigger loans have lower interest rates, while credit cards have outrageous interest rates. For example: a $10,000 credit card, maxed out, with an APR of 20% will generate an estimate of $168 interest a month, while an $8,000 maxed out credit card with an interest rate of 28% will generate an estimate of $188 a month. This means that even if the balance that needs repaying is lower, your money will not go there, but to the bank, instead, as interest. You will end up paying the bank and not getting rid of debt.

Keep all your repayments at the minimum monthly amount, except the one with the highest APR. Redirect every available dollar there. Once it has been repaid, start over with the remaining ones. Again, choose the loan with the highest interest rate, only this time, use your available funds and the amount you paid as interest for the loan you just escaped from. Repeat this over and over again. If the first 3 credit cards or loans will be easily managed, the temptation rises with the next ones, because the amount of money used for monthly payments will increase. You may sometimes say to yourself "I could pay less and use the money for something you don't actually need". Eliminate this way of thinking, because you have made it a priority to release yourself from financial strain.

While fighting the battle of getting yourself out of debt, misfortune may come in one way or the other, we are going to look at a particular situation in case you become unemployed at this time.

There is never a good time to find you unemployed, but in today's economy it seems unemployment can strike anyone at any time. Naturally you cut out any unnecessary expenses and tightened your financial belt, but you may still be worried about paying your debts without falling behind and paying late fees and more interest.

Analyze your creditors and Prioritize- Make a list of all your debts and their monthly payments. Use this list to create a budget and see what you can pay with any severance payments or unemployment benefits. Then prioritize your list. Ideally, you should try to spread the money you do have around, paying a bit to all of your creditors rather than skipping payments completely. Making at least the minimum payments each month will protect your credit score. Depending on how much debt you have, however, you may not be able to keep all of your payments current. Know which payments are most important, just in case.

Enter an arrangement with your creditors -Now that you have looked at a list of your creditors and your budget, it's time to pick up the phone. Call your creditors right away and explain your situation to them. Ask if they can work with you to lower your interest rate or your monthly payment. Perhaps they can consolidate multiple debts into one smaller payment for you. Creditors would much rather get some of what you owe them than none, frequently making them willing to work with debtors who are struggling financially.

Consult a credit counselor- Contact a reputable credit counseling agency for professional help managing your debt. A credit counselor will help you figure out how to make ends meet and may be able to work with creditors on your behalf and get a better deal than you could on your own. Some agencies are nonprofit while others charge for this service.

Though it may seem counter-intuitive to pay for help when money is already tight, the investment is well worth the credit protection and peace of mind these organizations can offer. Just make sure you are working with a reputable, qualified credit counselor. If the deal they offer seems too good to be true, it probably is.

Unemployment is a scary time, but you can get through it and manage your debt when you tackle the problem early on and get the right help. It may take a year, three or even more. But remember that if you follow these steps to becoming debt free, as hard as it may seem, you will succeed. When you balance 3 years of efforts with a lifetime of knowing you OWN your money, guess who the winner is!

Dealing With the Debts of Someone Who Has Died

In case your spouse or a partner dies, their debts don't necessarily become discharged. But who has to pay them and when do they not have to be paid by the estate of the deceased?

Joint debts and individual debt -Joint debts are where two or more people are responsible for the full debt. It's usual practice for the survivor to be responsible for the payment of any outstanding amount.

An individual debt is owed by one person and is in their name only.

You do not need to worry about a lot about outstanding debts just knowing what to do will bring great relief.

Joint debts - There may be some insurance to settle the debt as is often the case with a mortgage, so check the terms of any policies that you have. In the event that there are no insurances, contact the lenders and ask them to check the terms of the loan and, if necessary, transfer all future bills to your sole name.

Remember that any account in the sole name of the deceased will now be frozen, so make sure that all regular repayments are transferred to an active account. Most lenders are sympathetic to such situations and will arrange to temporarily freeze interest on debts or renegotiate the repayments. Some banking institutions like credit unions have insurance policies which take care of joint loans. The deceased portion is frozen and paid for by the insurance policy and his/her savings paid to the heir. This sounds interesting.

Individual debts - In the case of individual debts in the name of the deceased only, contact the lender to notify them of the death. You will need to provide a letter showing details of the debt to whoever is dealing with the deceased person's estate.

Some personal protection insurance (PPI) policies include life cover which will pay out in the event of the death of the borrower so it's worth checking the terms of such insurances with the lender. Sometimes credit cards are covered by an element of PPI, so it's worth checking if life insurance is included. Note that there is always a time frame to submit the death report for this debt cancellation.

It's not uncommon to receive demands and requests for payment from credit card companies and lenders even after you've informed them that the debtor is deceased. This is usually due to delays in updating computer records. Make sure you have informed interested parties of the person's death and if let them know that you are in the process of dealing with the estate.

Dealing with the affairs of a close relative or friend who has died is never easy. If you are approached to be an executor on someone's will while they are still living, try to ensure that all the necessary paperwork is in order and that any insurances are up to date to make the process as smooth as possible after they have gone.

Consider Debt relief

No matter where you are on the borrowing spectrum, a strategic debt management plan can either increase your cash flow or reduce the amount of interest you pay. In some cases, it can do both. Having no plan at all, however, will only cost you time and money.

If you are struggling with debt, don't panic. Plenty of people are in the same position as you and there are multiple resources available to help. Below, we take a look at some of the best debt relief options.

Debt Settlement Companies- There's an amazing number of debt settlement companies ready to help people who are struggling to pay back credit cards, loans and mortgages. They'll represent you when negotiating with lenders. These companies will work on your behalf to cut down on the balance owed, eliminate fees and obtain reduced interest rates. Make a simulation of the trade off point between the company's fees and the value of benefit to be obtained from the loan repayment. There are companies with outrageous fees, beware of such companies.

Don't walk into a credit counselor or trustee's office with your eyes closed. It is critical that you are fully aware of how these companies are compensated and on whose best interest they base their advice.

In my experience as a finance professional, I have come across too many people who were so embarrassed and anguished over the state of their finances that they took the first piece of bankruptcy or consolidation advice they were given without considering, or even understanding, the ramifications. As a result, they damaged their credit for longer than necessary, paid higher fees than they should have, and enriched unscrupulous companies who specialize in preying on overextended and overwhelmed people.

Non-Profit Credit Counseling- While debt settlement companies typically charge a fee for their services, this is not the case with many credit counselors. You can take advantage of the free services from a credit counselor in person, online or over the phone. Such counseling programs exist at credit unions, universities, military bases and even housing authorities.

The theme of the advice listed above is to be proactive. Take control of your debt situation before it completely takes over your life. Doing nothing is the worst possible thing that you can do. Reach out for help today so that you can start working towards a life without the burden of debt.

Consult With an Attorney - An attorney will offer invaluable advice about how to get out of debt. Find an attorney who has experience representing debtors. If you retain his services, all correspondence from your creditors will be channeled through his office. He'll likely know a few tricks that will reduce the amount that you owe, spur the creditors to accept a settlement or even stop pursuing the debt.

Budgeting Spreadsheet- Be proactive and micromanage your personal finances with a budgeting spreadsheet. While many people think that these programs are only for large organizations, they also help individuals get their finances in order so that they can emerge from debt. It's easier and quicker than keeping track of expenses in an old fashioned checkbook.

Chapter Five
Retirement Planning

Retirement is a major must in the battle of life. If we live long enough, we'll eventually reach a point where we either leave our careers and businesses or finish working for a living altogether. There was a time when companies included pension plans in their compensation packages and employees could look forward to receiving a percentage of their salaries to live on for the rest of their lives. In Africa and other Emerging economies, where there is a ceiling and the amount you can receive as social security benefits, social security benefits are not enough to offset the cost of living, so a person cannot retire based on Social Security income alone.

It's up to the individual to create a comfortable retirement for him or herself. It's a good idea to do as much as possible to ensure that you will have a secure and enjoyable retirement.

Learning precisely how to do that can be daunting. Speaking with a Financial Planner can certainly help, but there are steps you can also take to help create a bright future after your working life ends.

Taking a closer look is key to your own retirement planning. Before you conclude that you've fallen short of retirement plans or that you don't dare spend an extra dime of your retirement funds for fear of running out, decide what you really need based on your own finances and expectations.

Consider yourself lucky that you are "planning" a retirement because many people around the world just accept what fate brings them upon retirement, if they reach that age. Your retired life will shape up basing on how well (or poorly) you have prepared yourself for that time. Most people retire at the age of 65; if you plan the same, depending on your health and habits, you may pass another couple of decades. Sustainability and satisfaction are the two most important aspects of retired life; you must have enough resources to cover all essential expenses and you must be content with how you live in retirement.

Whether you're 18 or 55, the best time to start saving for retirement was yesterday. The fact is, if you're earning an income at all, some of that income should be put away for your future. Knowing your options, and how to take advantage of the retirement savings vehicles available to you can help you be prepared when you do finally decide to retire.

Make a Plan for Retirement- Saving for retirement can be a very difficult thing to figure out at first. If you need to get a handle on what you need to do to create a large basket, you need to begin with a plan. You need to start by establishing your net worth (the total value of your assets minus the value of your debts (things like the value of your house minus the value of what you still owe on your mortgage. Don't be perturbed if your debts outweigh your assets. Even if you find your net worth is negative (as many people do), start there to figure out what you can do to make it positive.

First, determine what you'll need to contribute to reach your retirement goal. You want a basket that can annually deliver between 80 to 95 percent of your pretax, pre-retirement salary. How much will you need to contribute to reach that goal? More importantly, how will you ensure those contributions are made?

Next, you need to create a budget of your recurring expenses and include your savings contributions as a monthly expense. A budget will also clearly show you where your money's going and should also provide some insight into what debts should be dealt with first. Now that a plan is in place, you are going to need to change your mindsets in order to stick to it.

Saving up for years just so you can make 80 to 95 percent of your old salary annually when you retire sounds like a astonishing idea. How can you save that much while you're still living your life before retirement? Fortunately, there's compounding effect feature- small amounts of money contributed to a retirement savings account like a 401k that can grow by leaps and bounds over the course of a few decades. Still, you have to sow in order to reap and when it comes to saving for retirement, it can be difficult to have the discipline necessary to pay now in order to benefit later. This is where a savings mindset comes in.

You should designate an amount of your pretax income to contribute to your retirement savings on a monthly or bi-weekly basis and have it taken out of your paycheck, just like your personal income taxes. It's easiest to save money when you don't have it in your hands; you're effectively taking the decision of whether to save that money out of your control.

Budget close to your retirement- **Create a budget you can stick to just before you retire. After years of creating and updated budgets, as your net worth grew more and more positive, you should be a personal professional at making budgets by now. This is not to say that you have to look forward to living frugally for the rest of your life, just wisely. What is it you've always envisioned yourself doing when you retire? If it's travel, then create a travel category as a monthly expense in your retirement budget. If it's spending time with your family, then create family shrill category.**

You can still live your retirement years the way you like; sticking to a budget will help keep you from outliving your nest egg.

You may have slashed expenses and saved for the last couple years. You've been good about not touching your basket. You diversified your portfolio well and weathered some harsh economic conditions, Now that you've reached the end of your work life, you must have created a substantial gold mine of fortune. Don't throw it away.

Get Long-Term Care Insurance – Death is inevitable to every human, sure, we are all going to die one day. We cannot say when or how but all I need to tell you is you will surely die one day. That is why it's a good idea to purchase long-term care insurance. This specialized form of insurance covers the cost of health care that extends long beyond a typical hospital stay.

On the surface, buying long-term care insurance doesn't seem to have much to do with saving for retirement. Remember, however, that smart saving also involves spending at times. With long-term care insurance, you're actually buying a policy that protects your retirement savings. Having to spend your basket on long-term care -- which can easily reach into the tens and even hundreds of thousands of dollars, depending on the quality and length of the care -- is not what you've been saving up for throughout your career.

Stretch your retirement Savings

Chances are, you have already started saving for your retirement. You either have an IRA or employer-sponsored retirement plan that you contribute part of your paycheck. However, as you become older and see how the economy is changing you start to wonder how you can increase your retirement funds. There are different strategies that you can do that will increase your retirement income.

How can you cut the IRS out of your retirement account? - Like many people, your tax rate will increase in the future. However, if you are eligible, you can start now contributing after-tax money to a Roth IRA or Roth 401K. The Roth accounts allow you to have a tax-free retirement income. Therefore, you pay your taxes now on the money you invest in your Roth account and the money in the account grows tax-free until you retire.

A second option is to convert your current or traditional IRA to a Roth IRA. When you convert deductible contribution to a Roth IRA, you will owe taxes on the money. However, if you pay the taxes now on your deductible contribution when you retire you will have earned more tax-free funds. Therefore, if you only convert the amount of money that will bring you to the top of your current tax bracket you will minimize the amount of taxes you pay to convert to a Roth IRA.

Keep Working after retirement age - After the retirement age, if you stay in the workforce, you receive a double benefit. First, you are not taking money from your retirement account and second you can continue to put money into your retirement account. Therefore, if you retire at the age of 68 instead of 60 you will continue to receive a paycheck for six more years. During this time you can still contribute to your retirement accounts. Even if you are out of the regular employee job, pick up freelance and consultancy positions and make some dollars from it.

Use the nest saving strategy - Before retiring, you should consider dividing your money into nests. The strategy divides your retirement funds into different nests that represent a fixed amount of time. Each of the nests will hold increasingly aggressive investments for later years. To use the nest system plan for a 30-year retirement. You divide your investments into 5 nests. Each nest represents 6 years of your retirement and the first nest would be invested in short, to intermediate-term bonds and money market funds. Your last nest can be invested into stocks or other aggressive investments.

During your retirement you use up one nest and will refill that nest with the next one. Afterwards, you will change the risk level of the nest to invest in short, to intermediate-term bonds and money market funds. The nest system ensures you have the funds each month for your current expenses and gives your long-term investments a change to earn higher rates.

Don't file for your Social Security benefits until you reach your full retirement age.

Delaying your Social Security benefits will increase the money you receive monthly. Therefore, the more money you receive from Social Security, the less money you have to withdraw from your other retirement accounts. Social Security will continue to adjust your benefits each year for inflation. By waiting until you are 66 or 67 to reach your full retirement age, you will receive 100% of your Social Security benefits. However, by claiming your Social Security benefits before your full retirement age will reduce your benefits by 25%.

Calibrate your saving- You may have received a memo to hoard a percent of your annual income (including any employer match) in your retirement account, starting with the first month of your career and ending with the last. That strategy not only lets you take advantage of the magic of compounding, but it also encourages the habit of saving and keeps your contribution level in step with pay raises. At the end of a 35-year career, you should have enough in the fund to see you safely through a 20- or 35-year retirement.

Assess your target

Retirement planners generally recommend that you have enough savings at the end of your working life to replace 70% to 85% of preretirement income. The targets take into account that you'll no longer be saving for retirement, getting dinged for payroll taxes or covering work-related expenses, such as commuting costs. To get you to an 85% replacement ratio, Fidelity recommends that you save eight times your final salary, minus Social Security and any pensions.

Some planners go further, suggesting that you aim to replace 100% of your preretirement income, on the theory that what you'll save in some categories, you'll spend in others. "Even if you're not paying payroll taxes, that cost will likely be offset by a new hobby or travel. Or if you're staying at home more, you'll want to remodel. There always seems to be something

But maybe your hobby involves reading by the fire, not skiing in Vail. Or maybe your mortgage will be paid off, or you'll move to an area where the cost of living is much lower than where you are now. Given that your biggest spending years are when you're raising kids, you might get along just fine with 60% of your preretirement income. A recent survey by T. Rowe Price showed that three years into retirement, respondents were living on 66% of their preretirement income, on average, and most reported that they were living as well as or better than when they were working.

McLeod's experience echoes research done by Erik Hurst, of the University of Chicago, and Mark Aguiar, of Princeton University. They report that people save on food costs in retirement not because they are eating less or buying hamburger instead of steak but because they have more time to compare prices and prepare meals. The time payoff extends to other activities, such as shopping for travel bargains or taking on household chores you might once have paid someone else to do.

Save Early and Often - When you are young, it can be difficult to put money away in savings — whether you are in college starting your family, or haven't landed your first real job yet, you're likely on a tight budget. If you are first starting out financially, be sure to open a savings account. Then, when you are able to open a ROTH IRA or 401K, or whatever account you choose, you'll have a little money to start with.

Diversify your retirement savings - Using more than one means of saving for retirement can greatly improve the lifestyle you can enjoy after you stop working. While you might have a pension plan already, you can diversify your savings by using different resources for saving. One example is the Registered Retirement Savings Plan. This financial vehicle allows you to set aside money for the future and provides investment opportunities that you can customize. Best of all, contributions are tax deductible, meaning you don't pay income tax on that amount until it is drawn on after you retire.

Consult experts - Investment professionals, banks and mutual funds all offer a wide array of services to help anyone to wisely invest their money or simply set up long term savings accounts. While it can be tempting to go it alone, it's in your best interest to utilize these services and get the greatest possible return on any investment you make.

Start Yesterday - If you've put off saving for retirement, you still have time to catch up. While the government limits the maximum amount you can contribute to retirement accounts each year, you can still make "catch-up" payments. Don't simply give up on the idea because you've waited until your 30's or later. If you aren't particularly financially savvy, a financial adviser can help you make a detailed "catch-up" plan that works with your budget. The best time to start making savings for your retirement is your last paycheck and not the next one.

The key objectives of retirement planning may be summed up as embarking the following areas of retirement scenery.

How would you live: Obviously, you would not confine your daily routine only to eating, sleeping, showering and watching TV just because you are retired? You need to be engaged with some kind of activities to stay healthy and happy; what you do throughout the weeks, months and years is how you live your life. The best retired life you can have is which enables you to do everything you enjoy on a daily basis. So, make a comprehensive list of your favorite activities and start checking how many of these activities your available resources may allow you to carry on.

Mapping your support network- Health and safety are the two top priorities of retirement; as we get older, sometimes help from friends, family or neighbors becomes inevitable. Nobody knows when some ailment or a crisis creates an emergency that is difficult or impossible to handle independently. The more people you are helpful to and in good terms with, the wider is your support network; if you have obligated someone with kindness, that person will be happy to come to your aid, should such situation arises. Moreover, easy access to hospitals, public transport and individual security are the things to look for.

Same home or new place: Taking a decision on whether to continue living in the same home or move to a new place depends entirely on the lifestyle you are seeking in retirement. Most people feel safe and comfortable in staying at the same place they always had been; most of the neighbors know you, your mortgage is paid off and nearby places that offer good value for money are known to you. But for the adventurous guy, pocketing the equity of the property, arrange a cost effective accommodation and use the extra cash for something desirable is more attractive.

CONCLUSION

When are you ready to start taking action on managing your personal finance? You have gone through this book and have learned some tips on how to manage your personal finance and how you can implement these steps to your personal life. It is never too late to start doing the right thing.

What you know will not change you but what you implement. Taking action is the key to transforming your finances. What matters is what you take action on at least an idea that can help change your life in the very instance. Delays and procrastinations are the number one destiny killers. If you think what you have read from this book can change your life, finance, work and family, just take the first step.

About 90 percent of our present position is based on our habits, good or bad. A habit is something that you do often and almost without thinking. Your great finance goal is to form good habits that function on their own, enhancing the quality of your finance life and increasing the scope of your rewards.

Make a decision today on what you will want your financial life to be before you leave this world. Set great targets on where you want your finances to be-make explicit written plans for their accomplishment. Create schedules and set deadlines.

Action orientation is the most outwardly identifiable quality of a winning personal finance story. This world is full of people who are always procrastinating –planning, preparing, forecasting and thinking of what is going to be done in the future. This will leave you worse-off.

The greatest virtue you can develop regarding your personal finance is a sense of urgency, learn the habit of moving quickly regarding a change in your personal finance, this will keep you to the front line in all areas of your life.

Nothing in your life succeeds as success in your personal finance. When you learn and apply these ideas on your daily adventures, you will develop a heated habit of success in other areas of your life.

Regarding your personal financial life you must have unbendable principles, have your time for everything, don't just flow with the wind and do not allow others set the pace in your financial life.

The ideas and rules in this book are easy to apply. They require the four Ds to make them part of your personal finance race.

Desire. This is the beginning of all great personal finance success achievements. You must the necessary efforts apply personal financial management habits until they become part of your personality.

Decision. You must make a clear, unambiguous decision that you are going to create a plan on your personal finance and stick to it no matter how long it may take.

Discipline. This will make everything possible for you. With a high developed sense of personal discipline, you can achieve financial success.

Determination. This is the most important value you can put in place to put your finances intact. It will help you to plough the road to success amidst pot holes, setback, obstacles and loss of income. Your determination accounts for the amount of believe you have in yourself.

There are really no limits on how you can succeed in your finance exempt for the lack if insights and the limits you place on yourself. *START NOW*

ABOUT THE AUTHOR

Manyi Tabot is a Financial Strategist, personal finance blogger and a creative writer. He is a social entrepreneur and a change agent. He is an Ashoka changemaker fellow, a semifinalist in Ashoka's Future Forward award for youth employment.

Tabot holds a BSc in Accountancy and an MBA in Financial Management; he is a wide reader in all areas of life and has worked as a Finance Specialist for several years.

He became incredibly curious about the way personal finance works, and while many people end up been frustrated with their finances. He began reading, researching and blogging on personal finance with a goal to bring to the light a course that is absent in all academic curriculum.

Tabot has written several articles on personal finance and has counseled several people on how to manage their finances.

He is the Co-Founder of Bestabo Foundation a family charity taking care of less privileged children (Ten percent sales from this book goes directly to the charity)

Tabot shares in this book, many years of research and valuable insights that can turn just any one from a financial misfit to a guru no matter the level of income.

He is married to Bessem with two kids (Daniel and Lois)

BACK COVER PAGE

The greatest unanswered question is why are people in the same career and business, earning virtually the same income having differently levels of financial success? Why do some succeed in their finances while others fail? Manyi Tabot has uncovered some answers to these baffling questions. In this self learning volume, he puts together a set of tips and nuggets that can transform any person into a personal Finance Manager.

This book will teach you to:

- Make savings for investments

- Create and run an emergency fund

- Control and cut down personal expenses

- Plan and develop a budget

- Plan for retirement no matter your age

Tabot provides a simple, practical, straight forward and easy to apply tips covering major areas of personal finance management.

As a result of the principles you will gather from *Insight to personal finance,* you will be transformed to a "prof" in personal finance and your finance security will improve.

www.ingramcontent.com/pod-product-compliance
Lightning Source LLC
Chambersburg PA
CBHW071802200526
45167CB00017B/1098